50
Things to
Draw &
Paint

Contents

Contents

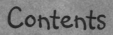

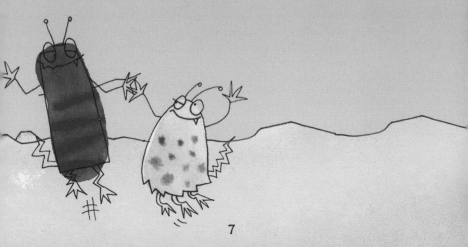

Scaly dinosaurs

1. Use a pencil to draw the outline of a dinosaur's body on green paper. Then, add eyes, a mouth, spikes on its tail, and toenails.

2. Draw a bony plate in the shape of a diamond in the middle of the back. Then, draw smaller plates on both sides of the middle one.

3. Draw over your pencil lines with a felt-tip pen. Add rows of U-shaped scales along the body. Then, add teeth with correcting fluid.

4. Draw lines on the bony plates on the dinosaur's back. Then, draw lots of little lines on the spikes and toenails. Fill in parts of the dinosaur.

5. For a dinosaur with a frill, draw several curved lines along its back. Then, join the ends of the lines with wavy lines, like this.

Painted flowers

It is shown here in yellow so that you can see it.

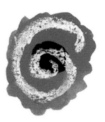

1. To make poppies, draw some swirly spiral shapes with a white wax crayon or candle, like this.

2. Mix some pink paint with water and paint it over the spirals. Then, add a black blob in the middle of each poppy.

3. To make daisies, draw some petal shapes with the wax crayon or candle, like this.

4. Mix some blue paint with water. Then, brush a rough flower shape over each daisy.

5. For tulips, use the crayon or candle to draw three or four pointed petal shapes, touching at the bottom.

6. Using yellow watery paint, paint over the petal shapes, like this. Then, leave all the paint to dry.

Fairy picture

1. Mix some paint with water, to make it runny, and paint a face. Then, paint a bright pink shape below it for the body.

2. Paint two paler shapes for the wings. Then, paint a shape for the hair. Add a circle for the wand, a little way away.

3. Leave the paint to dry completely. Then, use a black felt-tip pen to add outlines to the fairy's head, body and wings.

4. Draw a face, then add arms, legs and lines on the fairy's hair. Then, draw a wand with a star on the end, like this.

Some other ideas

1. Try different hairstyles. Paint a tall shape for piled-up hair, zigzags for spiky hair and curly lines for wavy hair.

2. Try different faces, too. A few dots make freckles, a round mouth looks surprised. Add round or pointed noses.

Fingerprinted horse

1. Dip your finger into black paint and fingerprint around and around for the body. Fingerprint the neck, head and ears, too.

2. Dip the edge of a piece of cardboard into black paint, then scrape it across the paper to print the legs. Add fingerprinted spots, too.

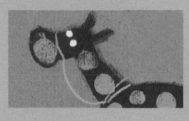

3. Print the eyes with white paint on the tip of your little finger. Then, draw the horse's reins with a blue oil pastel or chalk pastel.

4. Use a thin black felt-tip pen to outline the body, and draw the mane and tail. Outline the eyes and draw dots on them, too.

5. For hooves, dip the end of a thin strip of cardboard into light brown paint. Scrape the cardboard across the bottom of the horse's legs.

You could paint a horse sitting down, too.

15

Pet parrot cartoon

1. Using a pencil, draw an oval for the man's head, a square and a line for his chest and an oval for his hips. Add stick arms and legs.

2. On the man's shoulder, draw an oval parrot's body with a smaller oval for the head. The shapes should overlap a little.

3. Draw a big, curved beak on the parrot's face. Draw a big, beak-like nose on the man's face. Then, add a mouth.

4. Draw eyes on the man's face and on the parrot, too. Add the pupils, leaving a little white dot in each one for highlights.

5. Draw feathers on the parrot and add the man's hair. Add the parrot's toes. Draw the man's suit and add his hands and shoes.

6. Draw over the outlines with a black felt-tip pen. Let them dry, then erase all the pencil lines. Then, fill in the picture with paint or pens.

Tree painting

1. Mix red and yellow paints to make orange. Then, paint it across the bottom of the paper.

2. Mix lots of blue paint with water. Then, paint it across the top for the sky.

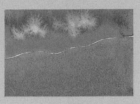

3. Before the paint dries, dip a brush into water and drip it onto the sky. The paint will spread.

4. Mix red and green paints to make brown. Drag your brush down to paint a tree trunk.

5. Add branches in the same way. Use a thinner paintbrush to add twigs.

6. When the paint is dry, add wavy lines for leaves with a brown oil pastel or wax crayon.

7. Mix some more shades of orange paint. Then, paint a leaf shape around each wavy line.

8. Paint little leaves on the tree and in the sky, to make it look as if the leaves are blowing around.

9. When the leaves are dry, use a thin brush to paint thin dark brown lines on the large leaves.

Patterned reptiles

Lizard

1. Dip a paintbrush into some blue ink. Then, paint a spiral for the lizard's body, like this.

2. Dip the brush into the ink again and paint a head and a front and back leg. Add three 'fingers' to each leg.

Paint a blue dot in the eye.

3. When the ink is dry, paint dots in thick green paint. Add an eye, then let the paint dry. Add yellow dots on top.

Crocodile

1. Use ink to paint a long wavy line. Then, paint over one side again, to make a shadow, like this.

2. Paint shapes for the head and legs. Then, when the ink has dried, add two eyes with thick white paint.

Add middles to the eyes with blue paint.

3. Paint yellow triangles on the body and outline its eyes. Leave them to dry. Then, fill the shapes with blue paint.

Princess painting

1. Draw a circle for a head. Add her face and ears. Then, draw the bodice and skirt of her dress. Add little shapes for the toes of her shoes.

Draw little spirals in the circles.

2. For her hair, draw lines on her head, then add a circle above each ear. Draw puffed sleeves, then add her arms and hands.

Draw over the lines when the paint has dried.

3. Draw a crown, then add patterns on her dress. Fill her in with watery paints. Then, go over the lines with a black felt-tip pen.

4. To do a princess peeking out from behind a bush, draw the head and dress leaning over slightly. Add her arms at an angle, too.

5. Draw a bush overlapping part of the skirt and arm. Then, erase the parts of the skirt and arm that are inside the bush.

6. Draw lots of circles for roses on the bush. Draw a spiral in each one. Paint your drawing, then go over the outlines with a pen.

Windmill painting

1. Mix some green watery paint. Then, mix two different shades of blue, too.

The water is shown here in blue.

2. Use a sponge or a clean brush to wet the bottom half of some paper.

3. Brush short strokes of one of the blues, all over the wet area.

4. Add strokes of the other blue and green. They will run into each other.

5. Wet the top of the paper. Then, paint a pale blue watery sky.

6. When the paint is dry, add green grass and two windmill shapes.

7. Use the tip of a thin brush to add lines for the windmills' sails.

8. Use green to paint leaves in the foreground. Then, add red tulips.

Oil pastel lizard

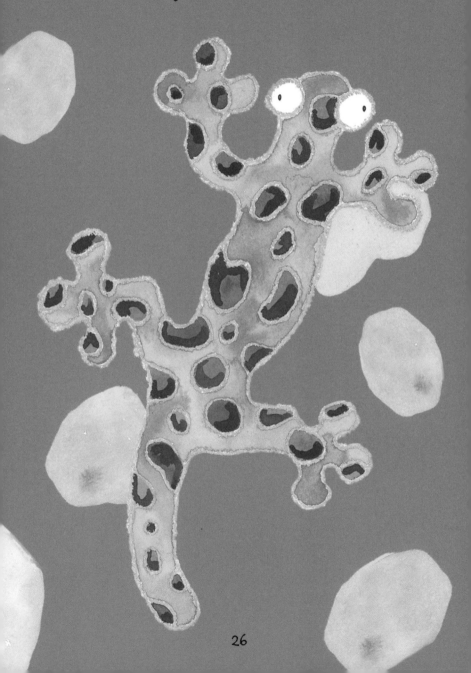

1. Draw a faint outline of a lizard with a pencil. Then, draw over the outline with a bright oil pastel.

2. Draw spots and blobs all over the lizard, like this. Make sure that all parts of the body are covered.

3. Dip a thin paintbrush into some bright ink, then carefully fill in the lizard's body, around the spots.

4. Fill in the spots with another bright shade of ink. The pastel outline will stop the ink from spreading.

5. Use a black felt-tip pen to add middles onto the eyes. Then, paint some stones around the lizard.

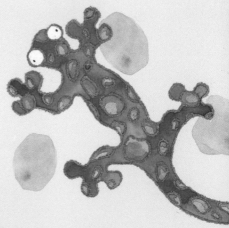

Inky shapes

The white shapes are shown here in yellow so that you can see them.

1. Use a white and a lime green wax crayon to draw a pattern of dots, circles and rectangles on thick paper.

2. Add a row of green lines, then draw more crayon shapes. Don't draw them too close together.

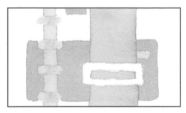

3. Mix turquoise ink with water and paint rectangles and squares over some of the shapes. Let the ink dry.

4. When the ink is dry, paint more rectangles and lines, overlapping the other shapes you have painted.

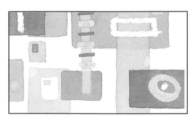

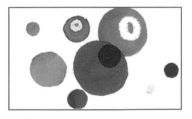

5. Finally, paint a few more rectangles with undiluted ink. Make them overlap some of the shapes, too.

6. To make inky spots, draw spots and circles with wax crayons. Brush watery pink and orange inks over them.

29

Elephant painting

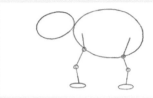

1. Using a pencil, draw an oval body and head. Draw zigzag legs with circles for joints. Then, add oval feet.

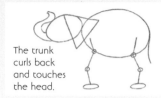

The trunk curls back and touches the head.

2. Add a triangle for the elephant's ear. Draw two curling lines for the trunk. Then, add a line for the tail.

3. Draw over the outlines with a black felt-tip pen. Add an eye. Then, erase any remaining pencil lines.

4. Dip a paintbrush into water and dab it onto the outline of the elephant's belly. The ink will spread.

5. Dab water onto other parts of the elephant. Spread the ink to make shadows on the body.

6. When the ink is dry, draw lines for wrinkles with a pen. Add curved lines on the knees and trunk, too.

Turtle picture

1. Use a blue pencil to draw the outline of a turtle's shell. Then, add a head, four flippers, a tail and markings on the shell.

2. Fill in some parts of the shell with watery turquoise paint. Then, while it is wet, add dots of darker paint. The paint will run.

3. Fill in the turtle's head, tail and flippers with turquoise paint. Then, add dots of paint before the paint has dried.

4. Paint the paper around the turtle with clean water. While the paper is still wet, dab patches of green and turquoise paint.

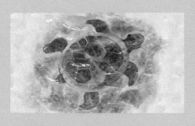

5. To make a watery effect, lay a large piece of plastic foodwrap over the painting, covering it completely. Then, leave it to dry.

6. When the paint has dried completely, lift one corner of the plastic foodwrap and carefully and slowly peel it off the picture.

Giraffe painting

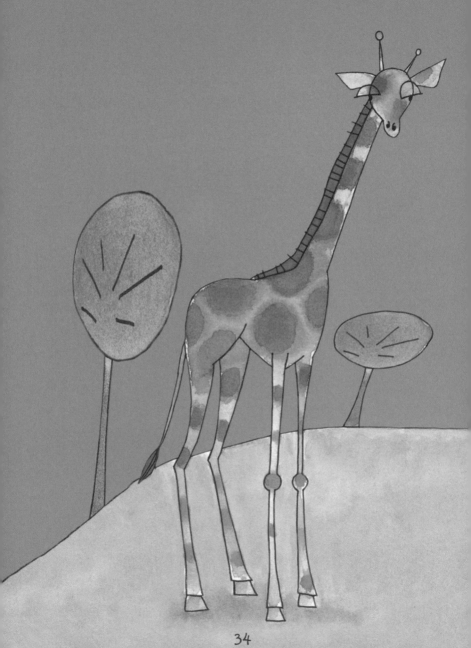

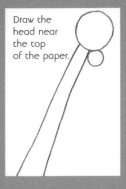

1. Using a pencil, draw two circles for the head. Then, add two long lines for the neck.

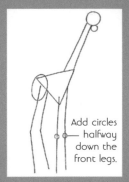

2. Draw a triangle and an oval for the body. Then, add four long lines for the legs.

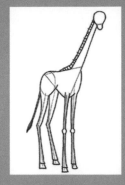

3. Outline the giraffe with a black ballpoint pen. Add a tail, hooves and a mane, too.

4. Draw eyes with big eyelids, then add horns, ears and nostrils. Erase any pencil lines.

5. Draw a hill and a tree. Then, mix some orange watery paint and fill in the body.

6. Blob brighter orange paint onto the damp body, like this. Then, fill in the tree and hill.

Blow-painted tree

1. Dip a paintbrush into bright ink and paint a big blob on a piece of white paper, for the tree trunk.

2. Hold a drinking straw above the ink. Blow through the straw, to 'chase' the ink up the paper for a trunk.

3. Then, use the end of the straw to pull a few thin lines of ink away from the trunk to make branches.

4. Blow the lines of ink with the straw to make more branches. Then, blow some thinner branches, too.

5. For the leaves, mix orange ink with some water. Dab the watery ink over the branches again and again.

6. Mix some more watery orange ink and paint grass around the bottom of the tree, like this.

Mermaid picture

1. Paint the sea along the bottom of a piece of paper with watery blue paint. Paint two shapes for rocks, above the sea. Let the paint dry.

2. Paint a shape for a mermaid's tail, overlapping one of the rocks. Paint a band for a bikini top. Then, add a tummy, face and hair.

3. Use a blue pen to draw around the tail and her top. Add her face with a black pen. Then, draw around the rock and add some cracks.

4. Draw one arm leaning on the rock and the other one waving. Draw scales on her tail and add curly lines in her hair.

Outline the shapes with pens.

5. For a diving mermaid, paint shapes for the tail, body, hair and face. Then, draw her arms reaching out in front of her.

6. Paint simple shapes for the body and tail of a fish. Draw around them and add an eye, mouth and fins. Add curly waves with a blue pen.

Pencil bugs

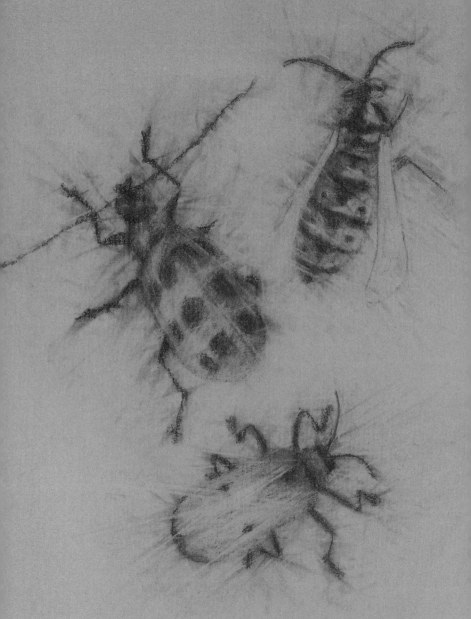

1. Use a pencil with a soft lead (a 6B pencil is ideal) to draw a bug's body, legs and feelers on a piece of paper.

2. Shade the body, making it darker close to the edges. Fill in the head and legs, then add some spots on the body.

3. Rub lines across the bug with an eraser to smudge the pencil a little. Rub the lines in different directions.

4. Using a harder pencil, such as a 2B, draw over the bug's outlines again. Add more shading and spots, too.

5. Rub more lines over the drawing, but be more careful this time. Smudge the lines a little.

6. Rub away some of the shading with the eraser, to create a shiny highlight on the bug's body.

Painted seals

1. Using a pencil, draw the outline of a seal's body on a thick sheet of white paper. Then, add the flippers.

2. Mix some blue paint with water, to make it watery. Then, fill in the seal's outline, using a thin paintbrush.

3. While the paint is still wet, lift off a line of paint along the seal's body with a tissue, like this.

4. Paint darker blue lines for shadows along the neck, flippers and tummy. Paint a shadow on the tail, too.

5. Draw an outline around the seal with a black felt-tip pen. Draw lines on the tummy and flippers, too.

6. Use the pen to add an eye, ear and nose. Draw some dots on the chin and add long whiskers.

Cartoon faces

1. Paint an oval shape for the face with watery paint. Paint a body below the face, then add some orange hair.

2. When the paint is dry, draw around the face with a thin black pen. Then, add a face and two ears.

3. Draw a few lines on the hair. Use curly, wavy or straight lines for different kinds of hair.

4. Draw a scarf below the face. Then, draw curved lines for shoulders and two lines for arms.

You could draw lots of people, to make a crowd.

Wax resist fish

1. Draw the outline of lots of fish with a yellow wax crayon. Add eyes, fins and different patterns on the bodies with the crayon.

2. Mix some watery orange paint and paint a line of orange on part of one fish. Don't worry if you overlap the outline a little.

3. Mix a paler yellowy-orange shade of paint and use it to fill in the rest of the fish. The wax crayon lines will resist the paint.

4. Paint the other fish, using bright, watery paints. When the paint is dry, add some little red or blue dots onto some of them, too.

5. To add watery splatters to your painting, dip a dry paintbrush into some dark blue paint. Then, hold the brush over your painting.

6. Pull the tip of one of your fingers across the brush's bristles. The paint will splatter all over the paper. Do this again and again.

Painted princess

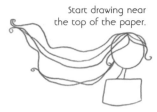

Start drawing near the top of the paper.

1. Use a pencil to draw a rectangle for the bodice of the dress. Add the princess' neck and a head. Then, draw lots of long, wavy hair.

2. Draw a little crown on top of her head. Then, add two shapes on either side of her neck, for a collar. Draw her eyes, nose and lips.

3. Draw one sleeve coming out to one side and the other one coming in front of her bodice. Then, draw both her hands.

Add long ribbons coming from the bow.

4. Draw the skirt of her dress with a curved bottom edge. Draw her shoes, too. Add a sash around her waist and a bow at the side.

Paint the bow the same shade as her sash.

5. Fill in her dress with watery paint. Mix paint for her skin, then paint her face, neck and hands. Paint her hair, shoes and sash, too.

6. Decorate her dress, sash and bow with hearts and dots. When the paint is dry, draw over the pencil line with a black felt-tip pen.

Printed birds

1. Pour some thick brown paint onto a plate. Then, dip the edge of a strip of cardboard into it.

2. Press the painted edge onto your paper to make a branch. Then, print more branches.

3. Use narrower pieces of cardboard to print shorter branches. Leave spaces for the birds.

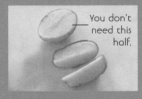

You don't need this half.

4. While the paint dries, cut a potato in half, along its length. Then, cut one piece in half again.

5. Spread red paint on some paper towels. Press the cut side of a small piece of potato onto it.

6. Print a bird's body on a branch, with the straight edge at the top. Then, print more bodies.

Twist the cardboard around, like this.

7. Print a tail on each bird with the edge of a piece of cardboard. Finger paint a head, too.

8. For the wings, cut a slice off the other small piece of potato. Print wings with orange paint.

Use a thin brush.

9. Paint a yellow beak and a blue eye on each bird. Then, add yellow lines for the legs and claws.

Painted butterflies

1. Pour some blue paint onto an old plate and mix it with water. Then, use a small brush to paint butterfly wings.

2. Rinse your brush. Then, while the blue paint is wet, dab small dots of green paint onto it. The green paint will spread a little.

3. Leave the paint to dry. Then, paint a dark blue body in the middle of the wings. Add thin feelers at the top of the body.

4. Paint lots more butterflies with orange and red paint, and pink and yellow, too. Then, leave the paint to dry completely.

5. Dip a dry brush into some runny paint. Then, pull a finger over the bristles, to splatter the paint all over your picture.

Inky panda

Make the paws shaggy around the edges.

1. Mix some black ink with water. Paint the panda's head and body, using a smooth, flowing line. Leave it to dry.

2. Use undiluted black ink to paint the ears. Paint a stripe on the chest, then add the arms and legs. Let them dry.

3. Use black ink on the very tip of your brush to paint little round eyes and a nose. Leave them to dry.

4. Paint the panda's eye patches in undiluted black ink. Leave a little white circle around each eye.

Use the side of the bristles, like this.

Let the stems dry before adding the leaves.

5. Mix green ink with water, then paint several sections of bamboo stem, with gaps in between them.

6. Paint leaves with undiluted green ink. Press lightly with the tip of the brush, then harder, then lightly again.

Pond painting

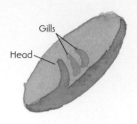

Gills

Head

1. Mix a few drops of ink with water in a small pot to make a watery ink. Use it to paint a simple fish shape.

2. Add more ink to the watery ink to make a medium shade. Add the head, gills and a shadow.

3. Dip a thin paintbrush or dip pen into undiluted ink and paint a thin outline around the fish, like this.

4. Use the brush or pen to paint an eye, mouth, three fins and a tail with undiluted ink.

5. Mix green ink with a little water and paint an insect's body. Then, add more water and add four wings, like this.

6. Dip a thin paintbrush or dip pen into undiluted ink and add a head, eyes, feelers and six legs.

Chalky landscape

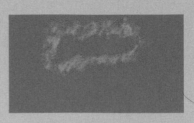

1. For the sky, rub the side of a blue chalk pastel on a piece of paper. Leave a space for the trees.

2. Add some patches of pale blue pastel to the sky. Then, add darker blue pastel over the top.

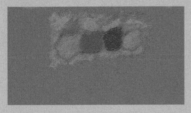

3. Use the side of an orange pastel to fill in a tree. Fill in the other trees with red and yellow pastels.

4. Add lots of diagonal lines on each tree with dark and light pastels. Let the lines overlap and merge together.

5. Use the side of green, yellow and orange pastels to create striped fields below the trees, like this.

6. Using the end of a black pastel, draw a line along the top of the fields. Add tree trunks and branches, too.

Horse painting

 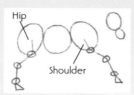 

1. Draw three ovals for the horse's body with a pencil. Then, draw two ovals for the head, like this.

2. Draw zigzag legs from the shoulder and hip. Add circles for the joints and triangles for hooves.

3. Draw the outline around the shapes. Then, erase any extra lines that you don't need.

4. Draw a pointed ear on the horse's head. Then, add an eye and a nostril, too, like this.

5. Draw two more legs. Add the hooves and outline the legs. Erase the pencil lines inside them.

6. Draw the mane and tail with short lines. Make them stream out, to show movement.

7. Mix blue ink with water to make it watery. Paint shadows on the horse, like this.

8. Paint the mane and tail with long flowing lines. Don't worry if you go over the lines.

9. When the paint is dry, outline the horse with a blue pencil. Leave gaps in some lines.

Moving animals

Rabbit

1. Draw an oval head with long ears. Draw a line for the position of the body. Add an oval body, an arm and a tail.

2. Draw several scribbly ovals where the legs should be. The legs are moving so fast they look like a blur.

3. Add motion lines and dust clouds coming from the legs. Then, fill in the rabbit with watery paints.

Flying duck

Make the wing and tail lines parallel.

1. Draw an oval for the plane and add a cockpit. Then, add diagonal lines for the wings and tail.

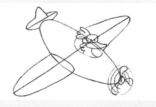

2. Draw the wings and tail. Then, draw a duck in the cockpit. Add a propeller with scribbly circles around it.

3. Add motion lines behind the wings. Then, fill in the plane and the duck with watery paints.

Fingerprint dinosaurs

Rub your finger around for the body.

1. Spread green paint on an old plate, then dip a finger into it. Fingerprint some blobs on paper for a body and a head.

2. Dip your finger into the paint again and fingerprint two legs. Use a paintbrush to paint a long neck and a pointed tail.

3. When the paint is dry, fingerprint dark green spines along the dinosaur's back. Fingerprint blue spots on the body, too.

4. Paint some little white eyes. When the paint is dry, draw around them with a felt-tip pen. Then, outline the head and add nostrils.

You could draw stripes instead of spots on a dinosaur.

5. Draw around the body and legs, going straight across the spines on the back, not around them. Add toenails, too.

Oil pastel face

Draw eyebrows, too.

1. Draw a head with a pencil. Add ears, eyes, a long nose and a mouth. Then, draw the neck and shoulders.

2. Add a line down the chin and neck. Then, fill in the face with diagonal lines of yellow oil pastel.

3. Add brown lines on one side of the face, mixed with more yellow. Add diagonal brown lines for the hair.

4. Fill in the whites of the eyes. Make the irises brown. Fill in the lips with short diagonal pink lines.

5. Add a blue background and green shoulders. Draw white lines on the left and dark blue on the right.

6. To finish your picture, draw over the original pencil lines again with a brown pastel, like this.

67

Seagull painting

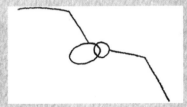

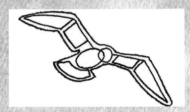

1. Using a pencil, draw an oval body and a circle for a head. Then, draw angled lines for the wings, like this.

2. Draw the lower part of the wings and a fan-shaped tail. Then, draw an outline all around the seagull.

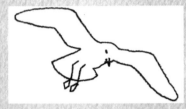

3. Erase the extra lines inside the outline. Add the eyes, beak and feet. Then, draw more seagulls.

4. Brush clean water onto the paper around the birds. Then, blob watery blue paint onto the damp paper.

5. When the blue paint is completely dry, use watery paint to add shadows on the birds, like this.

6. Paint the eyes, tips of the wings and tails with black paint. Then, fill in the beaks and feet with orange paint.

Cartoon dogs

Snooty pooch

1. Draw a bean-shaped head. Add eyes, a nose and a mouth. Then, draw a cloud shape for fur, and a line and fur for an ear.

2. Draw a long bean shape for the body and add a cloud shape at the bottom. Add stick legs with paws, and a line for the tail.

3. Add more cloud shapes for fur around the neck, on the legs and on the end of the tail. Then, fill in the dog with felt-tip pens.

Scruffy mongrel

1. Draw an oval for the dog's head, then add an oval snout. Draw lines and ovals for the ears, then add the nose and tongue.

2. Draw the dog's body. Add four stick legs and a curved stick tail. Then, draw shaggy fur on the ears and covering the eyes.

3. Draw some more shaggy fur on the rest of the body and the tail. Add some fur on the snout, then fill in the dog with felt-tip pens.

Seal and fish picture

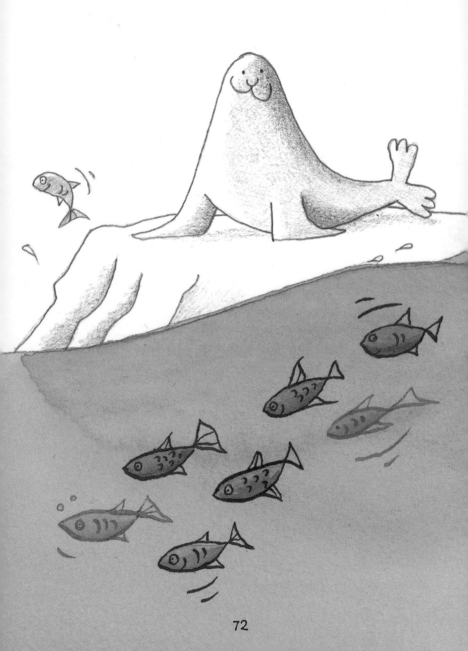

Seal

Erase the lines that overlap the flippers and tail.

1. Draw a big teardrop shape for the seal's body. Then, add flippers and a tail. Draw a face, too.

Add some lines on the tail, too.

2. Shade the body by pressing lightly with a pencil and filling in the shape. Leave the light areas white.

3. For shadows, shade over parts of the back, tummy and tail again. Make some parts really dark, like this.

Fish

1. Mix blue ink with lots of water to make it watery. Then, paint several oval bodies for the fish.

The two shades will blend together on the damp paper.

2. Add more ink, to make the watery ink darker. While the bodies are damp, paint a shadow on their tummies.

3. When the ink is totally dry, use a blue ink pen or felt-tip pen to draw outlines, fins, faces and scales.

Snail prints

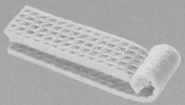

1. Cut a long strip of kitchen sponge cloth, and two pieces that are a little shorter. Lay them together, matching the top edges.

2. Cut a long piece of tape, and put it to one side. Fold the end of the long piece of sponge over the end of the shorter pieces.

3. Roll up the pieces of sponge, carefully but not too tightly, keeping the edges even. Secure the sponge with the tape.

4. Pour some thick blue paint onto an old plate and spread it out a little. Then, dip the end of the rolled sponge into the paint.

5. Print spirals all over a piece of paper. After printing each shell, press the sponge back into the paint again to make a clear print.

6. When the paint is dry, paint an orange snail's body below each spiral. Then, use a thin paintbrush to paint the feelers.

Sheep painting

1. Use a white oil pastel to draw ovals for the sheep's bodies on a piece of paper. They are shown here in yellow so you can see them.

2. Use the white oil pastel to draw horizontal lines below the sheep's bodies. Make some lines thinner than others.

3. Mix purple and pink paints with water. Then, brush lots of paint over the picture. The oil pastel shapes will resist the paint.

4. Hold the paper and gently tilt it from side to side so that the two shades of paint blend together. Then, leave the paint to dry.

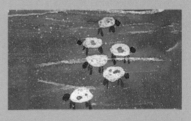

5. Mix some dark blue paint or ink and paint a little oval at the end of each sheep's body for a head. Then, paint four stick legs and a tail.

6. Dip a dry paintbrush into thick white paint, then pull a finger across the bristles, to splatter snow over the sheep. Let the paint dry.

Flower painting

1. Using a brush, paint a vase with thick paint. When the paint is dry, finger paint some dots on the vase.

2. For a daffodil, dip a fingertip in yellow paint. Drag six petal shapes, so that they join in the middle.

3. Add more daffodils. Then, when the paint is dry, finger paint a star in the middle of the petals.

4. For a tulip, finger paint a curved line with red paint. Add another line, joining the first one at the bottom.

5. For the blue flowers, dip a fingertip in paint and print a small dot. Add lots more dots in a triangular shape.

6. To finish the picture, use a paintbrush to paint green leaves in the spaces between the flowers.

Inky beetle

1. Using ink, paint a large rectangle. When it's dry, draw an oval with an orange chalk pastel.

2. Fill in around the oval with a blue pastel. Smudge it over the paper with your finger.

3. Dip a paintbrush or dip pen into some pink ink and draw a simple outline of a beetle.

4. Draw eyes and feelers. Add 'toes' at the end of the legs, and patterns for the wings.

5. While the ink is still wet, smudge it across the body and along the legs with a fingertip.

6. Put your picture onto a newspaper. Flick a paintbrush to splatter ink over the beetle.

7. Fill in parts of the beetle with a gold pen. Then, draw pastel dots on the wings.

8. Use a thin pen or a dip pen to write words around the beetle. Use flowing lettering.

9. Smudge the pastel dots on the body. Decorate the frame with pastels and gold pen.

Daisy picture

1. Cut two small pieces of thick cardboard. To print the daisies, dip the edge of one piece into white paint. Press it onto a piece of paper.

2. Print lots more white lines across each other, to make the petals. Then, paint a yellow dot in the middle of each daisy.

3. Dip the long edge of the other piece of cardboard into yellow paint, to print some dandelions. Then, paint dark green stalks and leaves.

4. For a dragonfly, dip a fingertip into some paint and drag your finger quickly across the paper. Then, fingerprint a head.

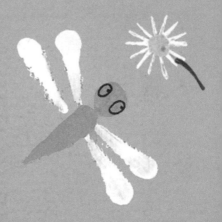

5. Wash your finger, then dip it into white paint and drag it to make four wings. When the paint is dry, add eyes with a felt-tip pen.

Ink pen cars

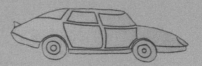

1. Pressing lightly, draw an outline of a car with a pencil. You could use pictures from magazines for reference.

2. Draw the windows, doors, wheels and hubcaps. Then, add the headlights and rear lights, then the rear bumper.

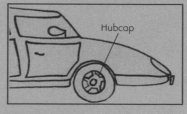

Hubcap

3. Using an ink pen, a dip pen or a black felt-tip pen, go over the pencil lines. Then, erase the pencil lines when the ink is dry.

4. Draw handles on the doors and add a bumper on the front of the car. Add a mirror, then draw shapes on the hubcaps.

5. Draw lots more cars from different views. Do some from the side, some front-on and some from the back.

6. When the ink is completely dry, use chalk pastels or felt-tip pens to fill in different parts on each of the cars.

Painted dog

Make sure you have lots of paint on your brush.

1. Paint a line of really thick black paint for the dog's back. Then, add another thick line for the head.

2. Use the edge of a piece of cardboard to drag the paint down the paper to make the head and body.

3. Use the corner of the cardboard to drag the paint to make the ears. Then, paint legs and a tail, too.

4. When it's dry, draw wavy lines under the head and body with a thin felt-tip pen. Add lines to the ears and feet, too.

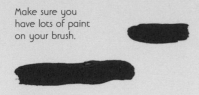

5. Draw a curved line for a collar around the dog's neck with a bright chalk pastel or oil pastel.

6. Use a craft knife to scratch vertical lines into the paint on the head. Scratch lines on the body, too.

Wax resist princess

The crayon lines are shown here in yellow so that you can see them.

1. Using a pencil, draw the outline of a princess in a ballgown on a large piece of thick, white paper. Try not to press too hard.

2. Use a white wax crayon to draw frills and patterns on the ballgown. Then, draw some wavy lines or curls for the hair.

The crayon lines resist the paint.

3. Using a thick paintbrush, brush water all over the paper. Then, dip the brush in very watery paint and fill in the ballgown.

4. Add some blobs or swirls in a different shade of paint to parts of the ballgown. The two shades of paint will bleed together.

5. Fill in the hair with more watery paint. Use a thinner paintbrush to paint the crown, face and arms. Then, add her feet.

6. Leave the paint to dry completely. Then, use a sharp pencil to draw around the eyes. Draw lines for the nose and mouth, too.

Monster scene

1. Wipe a damp sponge over a piece of thick white paper, to dampen it.

2. While the paper is still damp, mix lots of yellow paint. Paint it on with a large brush.

3. While it is still damp, brush on a darker shade of paint. The paints will bleed together.

4. Wait for the background to dry completely, then paint a blob of bright paint.

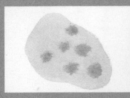

5. While the blob is wet, add little dots of darker paint. The paints will run a little.

6. When the paint is dry, draw eyes with a black felt-tip pen. Add an outline, too.

7. Draw some antennae, then add arms and legs, and a tail and fangs.

8. Add more monsters to the scene. Then, use black felt-tip pen to outline the background.

Blow-painted face

1. Mix two shades of paint with some water, to make the paint runny.

2. Pour a little of each paint onto a piece of paper, so that they touch.

3. Hold a drinking straw above the middle of the paint and blow very hard.

4. As you blow, 'chase' the paint from the middle to make spiked shapes.

5. Blow the paint lots more, to make it spread out in different directions.

6. Gently dab the middle of the paint with the corner of a damp rag.

7. Go around and around, to wipe the paint into the shape of a face.

8. Leave the paint until it is dry. Then, add a pair of eyes with a thin paintbrush.

9. Paint eyebrows and a nose. Then, add thin lips and pointed ears.

Wax resist flowers

1. Using a red wax crayon, draw some flowers near the bottom of a piece of white paper. Draw smaller flowers above them.

2. Add more flowers, using pink and yellow crayons. Then, pour some green paint onto an old plate and mix it with some water.

3. To add grass, brush the green watery paint over the flowers, like this. Leave a space at the top of the paper for the sky.

4. Fill in the sky with blue watery paint. Then, when all the paint is dry, add stalks on the flowers with dark green paint.

Scary fish picture

1. Mix thick red and white paints to make pink, then paint two curves with a thick paintbrush. Cross them over.

2. When the paint is dry, use a white pencil to outline the brushstrokes. Add lines for the fins and the tail, too.

3. Dip the end of a strip of thin cardboard into thick white paint, then print a row of teeth on each jaw.

4. Finger paint spots with pale pink paint, then add a white eye. When the paint is dry, add a black dot in the eye.

5. For a smaller fish, paint a curved brushstroke with a thick paintbrush, lifting the brush off quickly at the end.

6. Add an outline and details with a white pencil. Finger paint a white eye. When the paint is dry, add a black dot.

Horse cartoon

1. Draw an oval head. Add a curved neck and an oval body. Draw lines for legs and arms.

2. Draw the ears and the mouth. Draw oval eyes and nostrils. Then, outline the neck.

3. Draw a curved neckline and add a T-shirt. Outline the arms and add hooves.

4. Draw curved lines for the jeans. Then, add details, such as pockets and a belt.

5. Add cowboy boots with heels and spurs on them. Then, add lines for the mane and tail.

6. Draw lots of lines around the boots for hay. Fill in the picture with watery paints.

Landscape painting

Use thick paints.

1. Roughly mix orange and yellow paints together, then paint curves on a piece of cardboard. Then, add pink curves on top.

2. Mix some darker orange and yellow paints together. Paint two hills across the middle of the cardboard and fill in below them.

3. When the paint is dry, mix two shades of bright pink paint. Brush a line of each one across the bottom of the landscape.

4. For the trees, dab lots of vertical brushmarks in bright pink along the bottom of the hills. Add some blue or purple trees, too.

5. Paint a purple curve for a road coming from the back line of trees. Make it get wider at the bottom. Leave the paint to dry.

6. Outline the hills and some trees with a black felt-tip pen. Then, add some shading on them with a black oil pastel.

Wax resist mermaid

Draw the head in one corner of your paper.

1. Pressing lightly with a pencil, draw a circle for the head. Then, draw a big wavy shape for the hair. Make it overlap the head, like this.

2. Add two short curved lines for her body, coming from the back of the hair. Then, draw a curving mermaid tail.

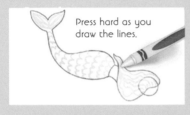
Press hard as you draw the lines.

3. Using a wax crayon, draw scales on her tail and wavy lines in her hair. They are shown here in yellow so that you can see them.

4. Paint the mermaid's face and body. Then, paint two arms stretching out from her hair. Paint small shapes for her hands, too.

The crayon lines will resist the paint.

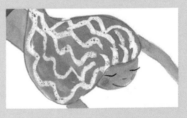

5. Mix some purple paint with water to make it watery. Then, paint the tail. Mix some brown watery paint to fill in the hair.

6. When the paint is dry, draw her eyes with a felt-tip pen. Add a nose, then draw her lips very close to the bottom of the face.

Watery picture

1. Draw a moon with a white oil pastel on a piece of thick paper. It's shown here in yellow so that you can see it.

2. Add lots of short lines under the moon, leaving a small gap. Make each line a little longer than the one above it.

3. Use dark blue watery paint to paint a line of distant hills between the moon and the reflection lines on the water.

4. Paint the sky and the water with watery yellow paint. Dab the sky with a tissue to lift off patches of paint for clouds.

5. When the paint is completely dry, paint a strip of land at the bottom of the picture with dark watery paint.

6. Add a tree trunk and some branches. Dab on leaves using the tip of a brush or a piece of sponge. Let the paint dry.

Ink and pastel dog

The ink will run on the paper.

1. Use a clean sponge or a wide paintbrush to dampen a piece of thick paper, like this.

2. Dip a thick paintbrush into some bright ink and paint lines for a body. Add a head, ear, legs and a tail.

3. While the ink is still wet, use the tip of a brush to add orange spots. Add one on the head, for the eye.

4. When it's dry, outline the body with a thin black felt-tip pen. Add a nose, eyes and lines on the paws.

5. Draw a few hairs and dots on the head. Then, use chalk pastels to fill in the nose and draw a collar.

6. Dip a thick paintbrush into some blue paint and brush it around the dog. Don't follow the outlines exactly.

Index

Written by Fiona Watt, Rebecca Gilpin, Anna Milbourne, Rosie Dickins and Ruth Brocklehurst.

Designed and illustrated by Antonia Miller, Jan McCafferty, Non Figg, Katrina Fearn,
Natacha Goransky, Katie Lovell, Lucy Parris and Kathy Ward.